Far Out

Far Out

60 exotic recipes from far flung places

Alain Schons & Gail Wagman

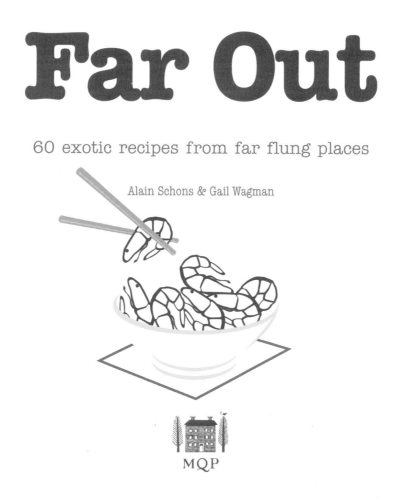

MQP

Published by **MQ Publications Limited**
12 The Ivories, 6–8 Northampton Street
London N1 2HY
Tel: 44 (0)20 7359 2244
Fax: 44 (0)20 7359 1616
email: mail@mqpublications.com
website: www.mqpublications.com

Copyright © MQ Publications Limited 2005
Text copyright © Alain Schons & Gail Wagman 2005

Design and illustration: Jo Hill
Photography: Gareth Sambidge
Home Economy: Fergal Connelly

ISBN: 1-84072-792-6

1 3 5 7 9 0 8 6 4 2

Printed and bound in France by *Partenaires-Livres*® (JL)

This book contains the opinions and ideas of the author. It is intended to
provide helpful and informative material on the subjects addressed in this
book and is sold with the understanding that the author and publisher are
not engaged in rendering any kind of personal professional services in
this book. The author and publisher disclaim all responsibility for any
liability, loss, or risk, personal or otherwise, which is incurred as a
consequence, directly or indirectly, of the use and application of any of
the contents of this book.

Introduction

This fabulous little book provides a taste of far-off lands, giving everyday dishes that special tang and transforming meals into a journey to an exotic location. For the price of a sprig of fresh cilantro, a pinch of garam masala, a splash of coconut milk, or some freshly grated ginger, you can afford to let your taste buds and your imagination take off.

Have you ever wondered what the secret is to making a good curry, stir-frying perfect crispy vegetables or throwing together a tasty Asian soup on the spur of the moment? Have you ever fantasized about surprising your family or friends with that extra special and exotic dish? Do you ever want to light up a dreary day with the smells and flavors of sun-drenched lands where bougainvillea and jasmine grow all year round? Or do you sometimes just simply want to add a little spice to your life and table? If the answer's "yes" to any of these questions, then this little book with its far out recipes from far away lands is just for you. So, get ready for take-off and bon voyage as you let your tastebuds do the travelling!

1

Out of Africa

Inspiration from beyond the Sahara

West African Summer Salad with Lime Dressing

In West Africa raw vegetables and fruits are used to make mouthwatering salads. Serve as an appetizer or side dish.

SERVES 6–8

1lb/450g white or red cabbage, or Chinese cabbage, thinly sliced
1 green or red bell pepper, thinly sliced
1 fresh pineapple, peeled and cut into bitesize pieces
2 tomatoes, cut into small pieces
1 cucumber, peeled and thinly sliced
2 celery stalks, chopped
1 small red onion, thinly sliced
1 fresh red chili, finely chopped, or 1 tsp chili flakes
2 tbsp unsweetened shredded coconut and/or chopped peanuts, to garnish
For the dressing
Juice and rind of 1 lime
1 cup/240ml sour cream or yogurt
1 tbsp sugar
½ tsp salt

1 In a large salad bowl, toss together the cabbage, bell pepper, pineapple, tomatoes, cucumber, celery, red onion, and chili or chili flakes.

2 To make the dressing, whisk all of the ingredients together until thoroughly combined. Pour over the salad, toss well to mix, and leave to stand for 30 minutes before serving. Sprinkle with the coconut and/or chopped peanuts to garnish.

Cook's Tip

To make a more substantial dish to serve as a light lunch or supper, simply toss in some leftover roast chicken or turkey.

Akara

Versions of these black-eyed pea fritters are found throughout Africa and the Caribbean. They are relatives of the Caribbean salt cod fritters known as acra, and the ubiquitous falafel that are found throughout the Middle East.

MAKES ABOUT 40 FRITTERS

2 cups/450g dried black-eyed peas, soaked in water overnight and drained
1 onion, coarsely chopped
1 hot red chili
1in/2.5cm fresh root ginger, peeled and chopped
1 large egg
2 tsp salt
3–4 tbsp water
Vegetable oil, for deep-frying
Relish, hot sauce or chutney, to serve

1 Working in small batches, tip the black-eyed peas on to a clean dishtowel and rub the towel over them to remove the skins. Rinse well in cold water to remove any remaining skins.

2 Put the onion, chili, and ginger in a food processor and process to make a purée. Gradually add the black-eyed peas, processing after each addition to make a smooth paste. Add the egg and salt, then, with the motor running, gradually add enough water to give a smooth, fluffy mixture that will drop from a spoon.

3 Heat the oil in a large heavy frying pan or a deep-fryer until a drop of mixture sizzles when dropped into the oil. Using two spoons, gently drop tablespoonfuls of the mixture into the hot oil, eight at a time. Fry, turning frequently, until the fritters are golden brown, then drain on kitchen paper. Continue with the remaining mixture. Serve hot with relish, hot sauce, or chutney.

Tanzanian Vegetable Soup

In peasant cultures, soup is often one of the pillars of home cooking. This hearty vegetable soup is no exception and is particularly good served with Akara (see page 12).

SERVES 6

2 tbsp vegetable oil
2 yellow onions, finely chopped
2 tsp ground ginger
1 tsp ground cumin
½ tsp ground cinnamon
2 carrots, sliced into ¼in/5mm slices
4 tomatoes, peeled, seeded and chopped
1 cup/225g fresh, frozen or canned
  corn kernels
4 yams or sweet potatoes, peeled and cut
  into bitesize pieces
½ cup/110g peanut butter
½ green cabbage, cored and shredded
  (about 4 cups)
1 cup/225g green beans, cut into thirds on
  the diagonal
Pinch of red chili powder or flakes, to taste
Salt
1 firm banana, peeled and sliced, and
  ½ cup/110g finely chopped peanuts,
  to garnish

1 Heat the vegetable oil in a large pan. When hot, sauté the onions until translucent, then add the ginger, cumin, and cinnamon and cook for 1 minute.

2 Add 8 cups/2 liters water, 2 tsp salt and the carrots and tomatoes. Stir in the corn and yams or sweet potatoes. Bring to a boil, then reduce the heat and simmer, covered, for 30 minutes. Skim when necessary.

3 In a small bowl, whisk together the peanut butter and ½ cup/120ml boiling water. Add to the pan with the cabbage, and green beans. Stir well and simmer for 15 minutes. Add the chili and adjust the seasoning to taste.

4 Ladle into bowls and serve steaming hot, garnished with banana slices and finely chopped peanuts.

Chicken Yassa

This is a typical tribal dish from Senegal. Traditionally it would be served spooned over a large platter of rice placed in the middle of a low table. Each person would then eat directly from the platter, using their hands.

SERVES 4-6

½ cup/120ml peanut oil
Juice of 2 limes
1 tsp ground turmeric
3 tbsp white wine vinegar
1 free-range chicken, about 5lb/2.25kg in
  weight, cut into 12 pieces
4 yellow onions, sliced
2 cups/475ml chicken stock
3 garlic cloves, crushed
1 tsp chili flakes
2 tsp ground ginger
1 tsp allspice
4 bay leaves
3 preserved lemons
3 tbsp chopped fresh parsley
Salt
1 lime cut into wedges, to garnish

1 Mix together ¼ cup/60ml of the oil, the lime juice, turmeric, and vinegar. Put the chicken pieces and onions in a shallow dish and pour the mixture over them. Marinate overnight in the refrigerator. Remove the chicken and onions from the marinade, separate and set aside.

2 Heat the remaining oil in a heavy frying pan or flameproof casserole, add the chicken pieces and brown all over. Remove the chicken, then add the onions and fry over high heat for 2 minutes, or until they start to brown. Add the remaining marinade with the stock, garlic, chili flakes, ginger, allspice, and bay leaves and simmer for 10 minutes.

3 Cut the preserved lemon peel into small cubes, discarding the centers, and add to the pan. Return the chicken to the pan, add the parsley, and simmer uncovered for 20–30 minutes, or until cooked through. Add salt to taste.

4 Transfer the stew to a serving dish and garnish with lime wedges. Serve with rice, couscous or millet, and vegetables.

Sausage Rougail

The word rougail is both the name of this stew from Reunion Island, off the coast of Africa, and the name of the condiment that is served with it.

SERVES 4–6

3lb/1.3kg smoked sausage, or fresh
  Italian-style sausage
3 tbsp oil
3 large yellow onions, finely chopped
4 large tomatoes, peeled, seeded and
  chopped
3 garlic cloves, crushed
1 tsp dried thyme
1 fresh red chili, seeded and chopped
Salt and freshly ground black pepper
1 tbsp fresh chopped cilantro, to garnish
For the Tomato Rougail
1 whole green onion, chopped
1 large garlic clove
1 fresh red chili
3 large ripe tomatoes, quartered
1 tsp finely chopped fresh root ginger
1 tbsp fresh cilantro leaves
½ tsp coarse salt
1 tbsp peanut oil
Juice of ½ lime

1 Pierce the sausage with a fork. Place it in a large pan with 8 cups/2 liters water and bring to a boil. Lower the heat and simmer for 10 minutes. Remove the sausage from the water and leave until cool to the touch. Cut into ½in/1cm slices.

2 Heat the oil in a heavy frying pan and sauté the onions over high heat until transparent. Add the tomatoes, garlic, thyme, and chili. Cover and simmer for 10 minutes, stirring occasionally, until the liquid is reduced by half. Add the sausage and cook for 20 minutes over low heat.

3 Meanwhile, make the Tomato Rougail. Pound the green onion, garlic, chili, tomatoes, ginger, and cilantro in a mortar. Alternatively, coarsely chop in a food processor. Add salt, oil, and lime juice and mix well. Transfer to a serving bowl.

4 Check that the sausage is cooked through, then season with salt and pepper to taste. Transfer to a serving dish and sprinkle with cilantro. Serve with rice, lentils, and steamed greens, with a little Tomato Rougail as a condiment.

Sweet & Sour Pork

The influence of North African traders can be seen in the spices used in this tasty sweet-and-sour dish from Cameroon. It is also very good made with beef or lamb instead of pork.

SERVES 6–8

¼ cup/60ml vegetable oil
4 yellow onions, finely chopped
1 tbsp curry powder or ras el hanout (see page 76)
3lb/1.3kg pork, cut into 2in/5cm squares
½ fresh pineapple, trimmed and cut into bitesize pieces
½ cup/125g raisins
1 (400ml) can unsweetened coconut milk
1 fresh or canned mango, peeled and cut into strips
Salt and freshly ground black pepper
Any combination of chopped peanuts, chopped hard-boiled eggs, chopped cucumber, unsweetened shredded coconut or fresh cilantro, to garnish

1 Heat the oil in a heavy frying pan or flameproof casserole and sauté the onions over high heat with the curry powder or ras el hanout, and 1 tsp salt and ½ tsp pepper, until the onions are soft. Add the pork and brown on all sides for 5 minutes, stirring frequently. Pour over just enough water to cover and bring to a boil. Cover with a lid and simmer for 45 minutes.

2 Add the pineapple, raisins, and coconut milk to the stew and simmer for 30 minutes, or until the meat is tender. Check the liquid level from time to time and add more if necessary. When the meat is cooked, remove from the heat. Add the mango and leave to stand for 1 minute, covered, until the mango is warm. Adjust the seasoning.

3 Transfer the stew to a serving dish and garnish with any combination of the garnishes. Serve with rice or millet and a little Tomato Rougail (see page 16).

Beef in Peanut Sauce

Known as mafé, this rich beef dish is served with rice all over West Africa (Senegal, Mali, Gambia, Ghana, Sierra Leone, and the Ivory Coast). You can use chicken, lamb, mutton, goat, or pork in place of beef if you like.

SERVES 6

3 tbsp oil
2lb/900g lean beef for stewing, cut into 1in/2.5cm pieces
2 large yellow onions, finely chopped
3–4 garlic cloves, crushed
1in/2.5cm fresh root ginger, peeled and finely chopped
1 fresh red chili, seeded and chopped
2 cups/475ml meat stock
2 tbsp tomato paste
1 cup/225g smooth or crunchy peanut butter
2 tomatoes, peeled, seeded and diced
1lb/450g small okra pods
Salt
½ cup/110g coarsely chopped roasted peanuts, to garnish

1 Heat the oil in a heavy frying pan or flameproof casserole and sauté the beef until browned all over. Add the onions, garlic, ginger, and chili, and cook for 5 minutes, stirring frequently, until the onion is transparent. Add the stock and bring to a boil, then reduce the heat to a simmer.

2 Add the tomato paste and 2 tsp salt, and simmer for 1 hour. Stir occasionally, adding more water if necessary.

3 Add the peanut butter, tomatoes, and okra to the pan and cook for 30 minutes, or until the vegetables are tender. Adjust the seasoning and transfer to a serving dish. Sprinkle with the chopped peanuts and serve over rice.

Cook's Tip

The okra can be replaced with any combination of shredded cabbage or bitesize pieces of sweet potatoes, carrots, and turnips.

Oysters Zanzibar

Europeans are thought to have introduced oysters to the East African kitchen, since there is no documented evidence that oysters were eaten by the peoples of East Africa before the Europeans arrived.

SERVES 6

36 oysters
½ cup/120g melted butter
4 garlic cloves, crushed
1 fresh red chili, finely chopped,
  or 1 tsp chili flakes
4 tbsp finely chopped fresh cilantro
¾ cup/180ml dry white wine
Sea salt and freshly ground black pepper
  to taste
1 lemon, cut into wedges, and Tabasco
  sauce, to serve

1 To open the oysters, wrap your hand in a dishtowel and hold the oyster flat side up in the wrapped hand. Slide an oyster knife or small, flat-headed screwdriver into the hinge end and move it back and forth gently, pressing it further in to prize the shell open.

2 Once the shell releases, drain off any liquid, and remove and discard the top shell. Repeat with the remaining oysters and place the half-shell with the oyster on a baking sheet.

3 In a small pan, melt the butter and add the garlic, chili, and half the cilantro. Cook over medium-high heat for about 2 minutes. Add wine and season to taste. Remove from the heat.

4 Preheat the broiler. Pour about 1 tsp sauce over each oyster, and broil for about 5 minutes, or until the oysters are just cooked through. Pour any remaining sauce over the oysters, and garnish with the remaining cilantro. Serve at once with lemon wedges and Tabasco sauce.

Egyptian Shrimp Pilaf

This Egyptian pilaf is an elegant
alternative to better-known dishes such
as Spanish paella or Italian risotto.

SERVES 6

2 cups/350g rice
6 tbsp/100g butter
3 yellow onions, finely chopped
2 garlic cloves, crushed
2 green chilies, seeded and chopped
½ tsp cumin seeds
2 cups/475ml fish or vegetable stock
1 tsp ground turmeric
2 tsp salt
6 tomatoes, peeled, seeded and chopped
½ cup/115g cooked or canned chickpeas
1lb/450g raw shrimp, shelled and
  deveined
1 tsp each chopped parsley and tarragon,
  to garnish

1 Put the rice in a bowl, pour over cold
water to cover and leave to soak for
15 minutes. Drain and rinse.

2 Heat half the butter in a heavy skillet
or frying pan and sauté the onions, garlic,
and chilies over high heat for 1 minute.
Add the rice and cumin and stir for about
3 minutes, or until the rice turns opaque.

3 Add the stock, turmeric, and salt. Bring
to a boil and then reduce the heat to a
simmer. Add the tomatoes and chickpeas,
stir, and cook for 15 minutes, or until the
rice is tender and most of the liquid has
been absorbed. (If necessary, add more
liquid during cooking but do not stir.)

4 Place the shrimp on top of the rice
and cook, covered, for 5 minutes, or until
all of the liquid is absorbed and the
shrimp are cooked. Melt the remaining
butter and pour over the rice. Sprinkle
with parsley and tarragon, to garnish, and
serve directly from the pan.

Senegalese Fish Stew

This is the national dish of Senegal, and
is a mixture between a soup and a stew.
Served with rice, it is a meal in itself.

SERVES 6

4 tbsp palm or peanut oil
2 sweet potatoes, peeled and cut into
  1in/2.5cm cubes
2 potatoes, peeled and cut into eighths
3lb/1.3kg fish steaks (such as sea bass,
  cod or halibut), about 1½in/4cm thick
3 yellow onions, finely chopped
2 garlic cloves, crushed
1 small green chili, seeded and sliced
1 (4oz/115g) can tomato paste
8 cups/2 liters fish stock
3 carrots, peeled and cut into quarters
2 turnips, peeled and sliced
1 slice yellow squash or pumpkin (about
  8oz/225g), cut into 1in/2.5cm pieces
1 small green cabbage, cored and cut
  into eighths
12 small okra pods, washed and trimmed
  (optional)
Salt and freshly ground black pepper
1 tbsp fresh chopped parsley, to garnish
1 lime cut into 6 wedges and rice, to serve

1 Heat half the oil in a heavy frying pan
or flameproof casserole and brown the
sweet potatoes and potatoes over a
medium-high heat. Remove from the
pan and set aside.

2 Add the fish to the pan and sear for
2 minutes on each side. You may need to
do this in batches. Remove and set aside.

3 Add the remaining oil to the pan.
Sauté the onions, garlic, and chili pepper
over a high heat for 2 minutes. Add the
tomato paste and blend well.

4 Add the stock, potatoes, and the
remaining vegetables to the pan. Bring
to a boil and then cook, uncovered, for
30 minutes. Season to taste.

5 Return the fish to the pan, placing
them on top of the vegetables. Simmer,
covered, for 10 minutes. Carefully remove
the fish with a slotted spoon. Ladle the
stew into bowls, placing the pieces of
fish on top. Sprinkle with the parsley and
serve with a lime wedge and steaming-
hot rice.

Banana Peanut Bread

The addition of peanuts gives this moist banana bread its distinctly African flavor. You can also add half a cup of chopped dates, raisins, dried apricots, or grated coconut to give it your own individual touch. If possible, make the bread the day before because its flavor improves with keeping.

MAKES 2 LOAVES

2 cups/300g all-purpose flour
2 tsp baking powder
1 tsp baking soda
1 tsp salt
1 cup/225g sugar
1 cup/225g softened butter
2 eggs
4 ripe bananas, mashed
1 tsp vanilla extract
1 tsp ground cinnamon
1 cup/225g peanuts, coarsely chopped

1 Preheat the oven to 350°F/180°C/Gas 4. Grease two 1lb/450g bread pans and lightly dust with flour. Sift together the flour, baking powder, baking soda, and salt. Set aside.

2 Put the sugar and butter in a large bowl and cream together. Beat in the eggs, one at a time, then stir in the bananas, vanilla, and cinnamon until combined. Gradually add the flour, blending well. Fold in the peanuts.

3 Pour the mixture into the prepared bread pans. Bake for 40–45 minutes, or until a skewer inserted into the center comes out clean. Leave to cool in the tin and transfer to a serving plate when cool. Serve with a fruit salad or fresh fruit after a meal, or with afternoon tea.

Malagasy Fruit Compote

This dessert is popular throughout the coastal regions of Madagascar and on neighboring islands in the Indian Ocean. The combination of sweet fruit and spicy chili might come as a surprise to your taste buds, but it makes the perfect finale to a spicy African meal.

SERVES 6–8

1 crushed dried chili or 1 finely chopped fresh red chili, or 1 tsp chili flakes
1 pineapple, trimmed and cut into bitesize pieces
1 banana, sliced
1 fresh mango, peeled and cut into chunks
1 melon, cut into chunks
1lb/450g fresh litchis, peeled and pitted, or 1 (15oz) can litchis
Grated rind and juice of 1 lime
⅓ cup/75g sugar (preferably cane)
Pinch of salt
1 tbsp vanilla extract
Dash of rum (optional)
2 tbsp unsweetened shredded coconut
Mint sprigs, to garnish

1 In a large bowl, combine the chili, fruit, and grated lime rind, and toss well.

2 Put the lime juice, sugar, ½ cup/120ml water, and the salt in a pan. Bring to a boil, and cook for 1 minute, or until the sugar has dissolved. Remove from the heat, strain and add the vanilla extract.

3 Pour the hot syrup over the fruit and then chill for at least 1 hour. Serve in individual bowls. Add a dash of rum to each one, if you like, sprinkle with coconut, and garnish with a mint sprig.

2

Oriental Express

Mouth-watering Chinese meals

Cold Sesame Noodle Salad

You could spend a lifetime sampling different variations of this salad at food stalls throughout China.

SERVES 4

12oz/350g Chinese egg noodles
1 tbsp toasted sesame oil
8oz/225g green asparagus, sliced into
  bitesize pieces on the diagonal
12oz/350g Chinese cabbage, shredded
1 cucumber, peeled, seeded and diced
1 carrot, grated
½ red bell pepper, thinly sliced
3 green onions, finely chopped
8oz/225g baby shrimp, shelled and
  cooked
1 tbsp toasted sesame seeds
3 tbsp coarsely chopped cilantro,
  to garnish

For the salad dressing
3 tbsp peanut butter
¼ cup/60ml light soy sauce
½ tsp chili flakes
3 garlic cloves, crushed
1in/2.5cm fresh root ginger, peeled
  and sliced
Juice of 1 lime
1 tbsp honey or sugar

1 Cook the noodles according to the instructions on the packet. (Be careful not to overcook them.) Rinse in cold water and drain well, then transfer to a large salad bowl, drizzle over the sesame oil, and toss to coat.

2 Steam the asparagus for a few minutes until just tender, then rinse immediately in cold water. Set aside.

3 To make the salad dressing, put the peanut butter, soy sauce, chili flakes, and garlic in a food processor. Add the ginger, lime juice, and honey or sugar, and process until smooth. Add a little water, if necessary, to make a pouring consistency.

4 Pour the dressing over the noodles and mix thoroughly. Add the asparagus, the remaining vegetables, and the shrimp, and mix well. Sprinkle with sesame seeds and garnish with cilantro. Serve as an appetizer or light lunch.

Stir-Fried Greens
with Shiitake Mushrooms

This instant stir-fry is incredibly easy to make. The greens should be barely cooked and slightly crispy and should retain all of their color. Serve as an appetizer, side dish, or with rice for a delicious light meal.

SERVES 4–6

1 tbsp vegetable oil
3 green onions, trimmed and sliced
1in/2.5cm fresh root ginger, peeled and
  finely chopped
3 garlic cloves, crushed
12 shiitake mushrooms, trimmed
  and sliced
¼ cup/60ml light soy sauce
1 tbsp honey or sugar
1 tsp toasted sesame oil
3 tbsp rice wine or sherry
2lb/900g fresh mixed greens (such as
  spinach, mustard greens, collard greens,
  bok choy, or Swiss chard), stems
  discarded
1 tsp toasted sesame seeds, to garnish

1 Heat the oil in a wok or large pan, add half the green onions, the ginger, and garlic and stir-fry for 1 minute. Add the mushrooms and stir-fry for 2 minutes. Add the soy sauce, honey or sugar, sesame oil, and rice wine or sherry, and bring to a boil. Cook for 1 minute.

2 Add the mixed greens and stir-fry for about 30 seconds until they become slightly wilted. Using a slotted spoon, immediately remove the vegetables from the wok and transfer to a serving dish.

3 Pour any sauce left in the wok or pan over the vegetables. Sprinkle with the remaining green onions and the sesame seeds and serve.

Stir-fried Vegetables
with Tofu & Cashew Nuts

You can use any seasonal vegetables in this tasty vegetarian stir-fry. Try green beans, broccoli, or asparagus.

SERVES 6

8oz/225g firm tofu
1 tbsp arrowroot or cornstarch
3 tbsp vegetable oil
1in/2.5cm fresh root ginger, peeled and
   finely chopped
1 garlic clove, crushed
2 yellow onions, cut into eighths and
   separated into layers
6 fresh shiitake or button mushrooms,
   sliced
12oz/350g snow peas, trimmed and cut
   into thirds on the diagonal
2 tbsp dark soy sauce
1 tbsp rice wine or sherry
1 tsp honey or sugar
3 tomatoes, cut into bitesize pieces
4oz/115g whole cashew nuts
Salt and freshly ground black pepper
2 chopped green onions, to garnish

1 Wrap the tofu in a clean dishtowel and place beneath a 2¼lb/1kg weight (a heavy frying pan filled with water will do). Leave to stand for 1 hour, then cut the tofu into ½in/1cm cubes.

2 In a small bowl, blend the arrowroot or cornstarch with 2 tbsp water. Set aside.

3 Heat the oil in a wok, add the ginger, garlic, and onions and stir-fry for about 2 minutes until the onions start to brown. Add the mushrooms and snow peas and stir-fry for 2 minutes more.

4 Add the soy sauce, rice wine or sherry, honey or sugar, and arrowroot mixture. Mix well and add the tomatoes. Cook for 2–3 minutes, or until the sauce starts to thicken. Gently add the tofu and cashew nuts. Cover and simmer for 2 minutes. Season to taste. Transfer to a serving dish and garnish with green onions. Serve as a side dish or as a main dish with steamed rice.

Simmered Stuffed Peppers

Throughout the world, you will find many recipes for stuffed peppers. This one is particularly unusual because of the mixture of meat and fish—a common combination in many Chinese dishes.

SERVES 6

4 dried black Chinese mushrooms
1 tbsp vegetable oil
12oz/350g ground pork
1 tsp salt
½ tsp freshly ground black pepper
2 green onions, trimmed and finely
  chopped
2 garlic cloves, finely chopped
1in/2.5cm fresh root ginger, peeled and
  finely chopped
1 tsp five-spice powder
1 white fish fillet (such as cod, halibut or
  sea bass), about 8oz/225g, ground or
  finely chopped
3½oz/100g cooked baby shrimp, shelled
1 tbsp soy sauce
6 bell peppers (red, green, or yellow) of
  the same size
1 cup/240 ml chicken stock

1 Preheat the oven to 350°F/180°C/Gas 4. Soak the dried mushrooms in a bowl of hot water for 20 minutes, then drain, mince, and set aside.

2 In a wok or large heavy pan, heat the oil, then add the pork, salt and pepper, and stir-fry until it is thoroughly cooked. Remove from the heat, then stir in the minced mushrooms, green onions, garlic, ginger, five-spice powder, fish, shrimp, and soy sauce.

3 Cut the tops off the peppers, and remove the core and seeds. Set the tops aside. Stuff the peppers with the pork and fish mixture and place upright in a baking dish. Replace the tops and pour the stock into the bottom of the baking dish. Cover with foil and bake for 20 minutes.

4 Remove the foil, baste with the liquid, and continue cooking, uncovered, for 20–25 minutes, basting occasionally, until the peppers are cooked. Serve hot with rice, or cold as part of a Chinese buffet.

Chinese Fried Rice

This is a good vegetarian alternative to the Cantonese-style fried rice usually found in Chinese restaurants. Serve as a main dish with vegetables or a salad, or as a side dish.

SERVES 4–6

2 cups/450g mixed vegetables (such as broccoli florets, sliced mushrooms, sliced carrots, sliced green beans, bamboo shoots, sliced bell peppers, peas or snow peas, bean sprouts)
6 tbsp vegetable oil
4oz/115g pine nuts
4oz/115g slivered blanched almonds
6 green onions, chopped
1in/2.5cm fresh root ginger, peeled and finely chopped
1 garlic clove, crushed
4 cups/900g cooked rice
¼ cup/60ml light soy sauce
1 tsp toasted sesame oil
1 tbsp chopped cilantro or mint leaves, to garnish

1 Prepare the vegetables: slice the carrots into sticks, the beans into thirds on the diagonal, the snow peas in half on the diagonal. Divide them into 2 batches: broccoli, mushrooms, carrots, green beans, and bamboo shoots; and bell peppers, peas, and bean sprouts.

2 Heat 2 tbsp of the vegetable oil in a wok or heavy pan. Add the pine nuts and almonds and toast them over medium heat until they turn light brown. Remove from the pan and set aside.

3 Add the remaining vegetable oil to the wok and stir-fry the green onions, ginger, and garlic for 1 minute. Add the first batch of vegetables and stir-fry for 2 minutes, then add the second batch and stir-fry for 3 minutes more, or until the vegetables are just tender.

4 Add the cooked rice and toss together, stirring frequently for 4–5 minutes, or until the rice starts to brown. Add the nuts, soy sauce, and sesame oil and toss to combine. Transfer to a serving dish and garnish with cilantro or mint.

Chinese Vegetarian Soup

This simple vegetarian soup can be made in no time. Appearance is important so the vegetables must be carefully cut and cooked to retain their color and bite.

SERVES 6

6 shiitake or dried Chinese mushrooms
2 tbsp vegetable oil
2 green onions, trimmed and chopped
1in/2.5cm fresh root ginger, peeled and
 finely chopped
2 garlic cloves, crushed
½ cup/125g Chinese cabbage, sliced
½ cup/125g carrots, cut into sticks
½ cup/125g green beans, trimmed and cut
 into thirds on the diagonal
½ cup/125g snow peas, trimmed and cut
 in half on the diagonal
1 tsp rice wine or sherry
1 tbsp light soy sauce
1 tsp toasted sesame oil
8oz/225g Chinese greens (such as
 mustard greens, collard greens,
 or spinach), coarsely chopped
½lb/225g firm tofu, cut into ½in/1cm cubes
12oz/350g Asian-style noodles, cooked
 (optional)
1 tbsp chopped fresh cilantro, to garnish

1 Wash and slice fresh shiitake mushrooms, or soak dried mushrooms in hot water for 30 minutes until soft, and then slice them.

2 Heat the vegetable oil in a large pan and stir-fry the green onions, ginger, and garlic with the mushrooms, cabbage, carrots, green beans, and snow peas for about 2 minutes until the vegetables just begin to soften.

3 Add 6 cups/2¾ pints water, the rice wine or sherry and soy sauce to the pan. Mix well, then bring to a boil and cook for 5 minutes. Add the sesame oil, Chinese greens, and tofu, and cook for 1 minute. Add the noodles, if using.

4 Ladle into bowls and garnish with cilantro. Serve as an appetizer or as a main dish, accompanied by a fresh salad.

Chicken in Oyster Sauce

This traditional dish is cooked in a heatproof Chinese clay pot. However, a flameproof casserole or heavy frying pan with a cover will work just as well. The chicken is cooked twice, making it particularly tender and tasty.

SERVES 6

4lb/1.8kg chicken pieces (legs, thighs
 and/or wings)
12 dried Chinese mushrooms
1½ cups/350ml chicken stock
4 tbsp oyster sauce
3 tbsp rice wine or sherry
1 tsp mild honey or brown sugar
2 chopped green onions, to garnish
For the marinade
1 tbsp soy sauce
2 tbsp rice wine or sherry
1 tsp toasted sesame oil
1 tsp chili flakes
1 yellow onion, finely chopped
2in/5cm fresh root ginger, peeled and
 finely chopped
2 garlic cloves, crushed

1 Combine all the marinade ingredients in a large bowl. Add the chicken pieces, toss to coat, and leave to marinate for at least 1 hour.

2 Meanwhile, soak the dried mushrooms in hot water for 30 minutes, or until soft. Slice the stems and leave the caps whole.

3 Preheat the oven to 450°F/230°C/ Gas 8. Put the chicken and mushrooms in a baking dish and bake for 15 minutes, turning the chicken once and basting with the marinade, until the skin is browned and most of the marinade absorbed.

4 Put the remaining ingredients in a Chinese clay pot or flameproof casserole. Bring to a boil over a medium heat and add the chicken pieces and mushrooms. Reduce the heat and simmer, covered, for 30–45 minutes, or until the chicken is tender and the sauce has thickened.

5 Sprinkle with green onions and serve with rice and Chinese vegetables.

Gingered Stir-fried Duck

Duck is widely used in Chinese cooking. This simple stir-fry is enhanced with the flavors of ginger and five-spice powder, giving it that unmistakably Chinese taste and fragrance.

SERVES 6

4 duck breast portions
2in/5cm fresh root ginger, peeled and finely chopped
2 green onions, finely chopped
1 tbsp dark soy sauce
2 tbsp rice wine or sherry
½ tsp five-spice powder
1 tbsp toasted sesame oil
1lb/450g snow peas, trimmed
1 tsp chopped cilantro, to garnish

1 Put the duck into the freezer for about 30 minutes until it is very firm but not frozen. Slice it into paper-thin slices and put in a bowl.

2 Combine the ginger, green onions, soy sauce, rice wine or sherry, and five-spice powder, and pour over the sliced duck. Mix together, making sure that the meat is well coated. Leave to stand for 1 hour.

3 Heat the oil in a wok or large heavy pan. Add the snow peas and stir-fry for 1 minute. Remove the snowpeas from the wok and set aside.

4 Add the duck to the wok and stir-fry for 2–3 minutes. Remove any excess fat with a spoon and discard. Add the snow peas and the remaining marinade, and toss gently. Cook for 1 minute until hot.

5 Transfer to a serving dish. Garnish with cilantro and serve with rice.

Cantonese Tofu & Shrimp

The combination of shrimp and tofu is a favorite duo in Chinese cooking. The subtle flavor of the tofu is a good counterpoint to the delicate taste and texture of the shrimps.

SERVES 4-6

½lb/225g firm tofu
1 tsp chili flakes
6 dried black Chinese mushrooms
½ cup/120ml chicken stock
2 tbsp light soy sauce
1 tbsp honey
3 tbsp rice wine or sherry
1 tbsp arrowroot or cornstarch
6 tbsp vegetable oil
1 tsp toasted sesame oil
1in/2.5cm fresh root ginger, peeled and
  finely chopped
2 garlic cloves, finely chopped
2 shallots, finely chopped
1lb 8oz/700g raw jumbo shrimp, shelled
  and deveined
Coarsely chopped basil leaves, or 3 tbsp
  chopped chives, to garnish

1 Wrap the tofu in a clean dishtowel and place beneath a 2¼lb/1kg weight. Leave to stand for 1 hour, then cut the tofu into 2 x ½in/5 x 1cm strips. Sprinkle with chili flakes and set aside.

2 Soak the dried mushrooms in a bowl of hot water for 20 minutes. Drain, then cut into slices and set aside.

3 Whisk together the chicken stock, soy sauce, honey, rice wine or sherry, and arrowroot or cornstarch. Set aside.

4 Heat 3 tbsp of the vegetable oil in a wok or heavy pan. Working in batches, stir-fry the tofu until golden brown on all sides. Remove and set aside.

5 Add the remaining vegetable oil and sesame oil to the wok. Stir-fry the ginger, garlic, and shallots for 1 minute. Add the shrimp and mushrooms and stir-fry until the shrimp turns pink. Add the stock mixture and cook for 3–5 minutes until the sauce thickens. Add the fried tofu, cover, and simmer for 2 minutes. Transfer to a serving dish, garnish with basil or chives, and serve with rice.

Mongolian Fire Pot

Along with Peking duck, this is one of the most popular and well-known dishes in the Chinese cuisine. The Chinese consider Mongolian lamb to be the finest, hence the name of this dish. Use a Chinese fondue set if you have one, or improvise with a large soup pot and chopsticks. Serve with hot rice.

SERVES 6

8 cups/2 liters homemade chicken stock
2 carrots, cut in strips
1 leek (white only), sliced
1 celery stalk, cut into four pieces
1 small bunch parsley, chopped
½in/1cm fresh root ginger, peeled and
  finely chopped
2 boned chicken breast portions
1lb/450g lean boned leg of lamb
3 fillets firm white fish (such as cod,
snapper, or sea bass), about 1lb/450g
  total weight
12 raw jumbo shrimp
For the accompaniments
3½oz/100g Chinese rice vermicelli
8oz/225g firm tofu, cut into bitesize
  pieces

6oz/200g Chinese cabbage, coarsely
  sliced
6oz/200g spinach, leaves cut in half
For the dipping sauces and herbs
Light soy sauce
Chili paste
Tahini, thinned to dipping consistency
  with water
Hoisin sauce
3 tbsp chopped green onions
2 shallots, finely chopped
4 tbsp fresh cilantro, chopped

1 First prepare the soup. Put the stock in a large soup or Chinese fondue pot and add the carrots, leek, celery, parsley, and ginger. Bring to a boil and cook for 15 minutes. Strain and set the soup aside in the soup or fondue pot.

2 Put the meat and fish in the freezer for about 30 minutes until they are very firm but not frozen. Once firm, slice the chicken and lamb into very thin slices, against the grain. Cut the fish into 1in/2.5cm cubes. Arrange on a serving platter with the shrimp.

3 To prepare the accompaniments, cook the noodles according to the instructions on packet. Drain and rinse them under cold water, and drain again. Arrange the noodles on a serving plate with the tofu, Chinese cabbage and spinach leaves. Put the dipping sauces and herbs in small serving dishes.

> **Cook's Tips**
>
> • Chili paste is available in Oriental specialty stores and large supermarkets.
> • A Chinese fondue set is perfect for this dish. It has wire baskets to hold the food in the hot soup, making cooking easy.

4 Bring the soup pan or fondue to the table and place over a lighted burner to keep the soup hot. Guests first cook the meat, fish, and shrimp in the hot soup, dipping them into the sauces and herbs, and enjoying them with the other accompaniments. When the meat and fish are finished, add the leftover ingredients to the pot and cook them for a few minutes, then serve as a soup to finish off the meal.

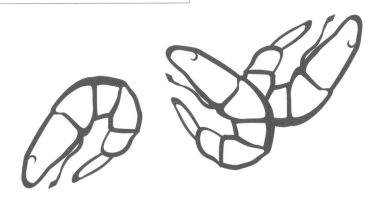

Beef Stew with Star Anise

Stews are common in the Chinese countryside but are rarely found on menus in Chinese restaurants. They require long, slow cooking but can be prepared several days in advance and reheated at the last minute.

SERVES 4–6

3 tbsp vegetable oil
2 garlic cloves, crushed
1in/2.5cm fresh root ginger, peeled and finely chopped
3 yellow onions, finely sliced
2lb/900g boneless beef (sirloin), cut into 1in/2.5cm cubes
3 tbsp Hoisin sauce
3 tbsp light soy sauce
4 whole star anise
1 tbsp mild honey or sugar
2 tbsp rice wine or sherry
4 carrots, peeled and cut into 1in/2.5cm slices on the diagonal
Salt and freshly ground black pepper
1 tbsp fresh chopped cilantro, to garnish

1 Heat the oil in a heavy frying pan or flameproof casserole. Add the garlic, ginger, and onions, and sauté over high heat until golden brown.

2 Add the beef and brown on all sides. Pour over water to cover and stir in the Hoisin and soy sauces, the star anise, honey or sugar, and rice wine or sherry. Simmer for 1½ hours, stirring from time to time to prevent sticking. Check the liquid level, adding more water if necessary.

3 Add the carrots and cook for another 30 minutes, or until the meat and carrots are tender. Season to taste.

4 Transfer to a serving dish, garnish with chopped cilantro, and serve with hot rice and Chinese vegetables.

> **Cook's Tip**
>
> Hoisin sauce is a sweet plum sauce that can be found in Asian stores.

Almond Cookies

If you are a cookie lover, this Chinese classic will be a welcome addition to your repertoire. Perfect served with green tea after a meal, as a dessert with a scoop of ice cream or fresh fruit, or eaten as a snack.

MAKES ABOUT 36

36 whole almonds
1 cup/225g softened butter
1 cup/200g sugar
1 beaten egg
1 tsp almond extract
½ cup/40g ground almonds
2½ cups/375g all-purpose flour
1 tsp baking powder
1 tsp salt

1 Preheat the oven to 350°F/180°C/Gas 4 and grease a baking sheet.

2 Place the almonds in a small bowl and add 1 cup/240ml boiling water. Leave to soak for 5–10 minutes. Remove the skins and set the almonds aside.

3 Cream the butter and sugar until smooth, then beat in the egg, almond extract, and ground almonds. Sift the flour with the baking powder and salt and gradually blend into the almond mixture.

4 Roll a generous tablespoon of the mixture into a ball and place on the baking sheet. Flatten the top slightly with your fingers and press a whole blanched almond into the center. Repeat with the remaining mixture and almonds.

5 Bake for 8 minutes, or until the cookies turn a pale golden color. Transfer to a wire rack and leave to cool.

3

Bollywood Feasts

Red-hot curries & soothing sweets

Cold Minted Potato Salad

Potato chat is a popular Indian dish. The juxtaposition of fragrant spices and potatoes gives it a definitively Indian taste, making it a perfect appetizer or side dish to serve with an Indian feast. To enjoy the flavors at their best, serve cool, but not chilled.

SERVES 6

6 red potatoes
1 cucumber, peeled, cut in half lengthways, seeded and cut into ½in/1cm cubes
2 tsp salt
2 tbsp lime juice
2 tbsp mint leaves, chopped
2 tbsp roasted cumin seeds, to garnish.
For the chat masala
1 tsp ground roasted cumin seeds
1 tsp ground roasted coriander seeds
¼ tsp freshly ground black pepper
¼ tsp red chili powder
½ tsp salt
2 tbsp water

1 First make the chat masala. Combine all the ingredients in a bowl to make a paste and set aside.

2 Boil the potatoes in their skins until cooked. Drain and cool, then peel and cut into bitesize cubes.

3 Put the cucumber and potatoes into a salad bowl. Sprinkle with the salt and lime juice and toss gently to combine. Add the chat masala and mint. Toss again, being careful not to break up the potatoes.

4 Refrigerate until ready to serve. Remove from the refrigerator 15 minutes before serving to release the fragrance of the herbs and spices. Sprinkle with roasted cumin seeds and serve.

Cucumber Raita

Yogurt and cucumber salads are commonly found on tables, from Bulgaria to India. It is difficult to imagine an Indian feast without one.

SERVES 4-6

2 cucumbers, peeled and thinly sliced
1 small tomato, seeded and chopped
2 cups/450g plain yogurt
½ tsp garam masala or curry powder
4 green onions, trimmed and thinly sliced
2 tbsp mint leaves, finely chopped
2 garlic cloves, crushed
Salt and ground black pepper
1 teaspoon roasted cumin seeds,
  to garnish

1 Place the cucumbers and tomato in a colander and sprinkle over ½ tsp salt. Leave to drain for 10 minutes.

2 Meanwhile, put the yogurt, garam masala or curry powder, green onions, mint leaves, and garlic in a salad bowl and mix well. Add the salted cucumbers and tomatoes and toss gently. Refrigerate for at least 30 minutes before serving.

3 To serve, remove from the refrigerator season with salt and pepper, and sprinkle with the cumin seeds.

Coconut Rice

Variations of this rice dish are found all along the southern coast of India and especially in Goa. It is a delicious accompaniment to meat and vegetarian dishes, and goes particularly well with Fish Caldine (see page 62), Dal with Cauliflower (see page 54), and Mixed Vegetable Curry (see page 56).

SERVES 6

2½ cups/450g basmati rice
4 tbsp/50g butter or vegetable oil
1 large yellow onion, finely chopped
½ tsp whole peppercorns
2 tsp ground turmeric
1 (400ml) can unsweetened coconut milk
1 tsp salt
3 tbsp chopped fresh cilantro,
  to garnish

Cook's Tip

Basmati rice is highly regarded for it's refined taste and texture, but you can use any fine long-grain rice, if you prefer.

1 Place the rice in a strainer and rinse under cold running water until the water runs clear. Put the rice in a bowl, pour over cold water to cover, and leave to soak for 1 hour, then drain.

2 Heat half the butter or oil in a heavy frying pan and sauté the onions over high heat until light brown. Remove from the pan and set aside.

3 Add the remaining butter or oil to the pan. When hot, add the rice, peppercorns, and turmeric, and fry for about 5 minutes, stirring continually.

4 Add the coconut milk, salt, and enough water to cover the rice by 1in/2.5cm. Bring to a boil, reduce the heat, and simmer for 15 minutes, or until the rice is cooked and all the liquid has been absorbed. Turn off the heat, cover, and leave to stand for 5 minutes.

5 Transfer the rice to a serving dish and sprinkle with the fried onions and cilantro.

Dal with Cauliflower

Pulses or dried beans are known as dal in India and give this dish its name. There are many variations, but this cauliflower version is a classic. It can be served as a main or side dish.

SERVES 6

2 cups/225g pink split lentils (masoor dal) or yellow lentils (toovar dal)
½ cup/110g whole cashew nuts
4 tbsp/50g butter or 4 tbsp vegetable oil
2 yellow onions, finely chopped
1 tsp ground cumin
1 tsp ground coriander
1 tbsp ground turmeric
1 tsp chili flakes
2 tsp freshly ground black pepper
Juice of 1 lime
2 tbsp grated unsweetened shredded coconut
2 cups/480ml vegetable or chicken stock
2 cups/475ml vegetable or chicken stock
2 tsp salt
1 tsp flour
1 cauliflower, cut into small florets
1 tbsp finely chopped cilantro, to garnish

1 Check the lentils for any loose stones or debris, then wash and drain. Set aside.

2 In a heavy frying pan, dry-roast the cashew nuts over high heat for about 2 minutes, stirring constantly, until they start to brown. Remove from the pan and set aside.

3 Add the butter or oil to the pan and sauté the onions over high heat until they start to brown. Add the spices and cook for 1 minute, then stir in the lentils. Add the lime juice, coconut, stock, salt and flour and mix well. Bring to a boil, then reduce the heat and simmer for about 20 minutes, or until the lentils form a thick paste.

4 Add the cauliflower and cashew nuts and cook for a further 10 minutes, or until the cauliflower is al dente. Transfer the dal to a serving dish, sprinkle with chopped fresh cilantro, and serve.

Mixed Vegetable Curry

Vegetable curries are a staple of the Indian diet and every region has its own specialty. This one comes from the coast of southern India.

SERVES 6

6 tbsp/90g butter or vegetable oil
1 large yellow onion, finely chopped
2 garlic cloves, crushed
1in/2.5cm fresh root ginger, peeled and finely chopped
1 tsp dark mustard seeds
Seeds of 4 green cardamom pods
1 tsp ground cumin
1 tsp ground coriander
1 tsp ground turmeric
2 potatoes, cut into bitesize pieces
2 carrots, cut into bitesize sticks
2 green or red bell peppers, halved and cut into thick slices
½ cup/115g green beans, cut into thirds on the diagonal
2 eggplants, cut into 1in/2.5cm cubes
2 small zucchini, sliced
1 (400ml) can unsweetened coconut milk
1 tsp sugar
3 tbsp chopped fresh cilantro
3 tbsp chopped mint
2 tsp salt
2 chopped fresh green chilies and/or 2 tbsp unsweetened shredded coconut, to garnish

1 Heat the butter or oil in a heavy pan or flameproof casserole, and sauté the onion, garlic, ginger, and mustard seeds over high heat for 2 minutes. Add the cardamom seeds, cumin, coriander, and turmeric, and cook for 1 minute.

2 Add the potatoes, coating well with the spice mixture. One at a time, add the carrots, bell peppers, green beans, eggplants and zucchini, coating each with the spice mixture as before.

3 Add the coconut milk and sugar. Bring to a boil and add the cilantro, mint, and salt. Lower the heat and simmer for about 20 minutes, or until the vegetables are cooked. (Do not overcook.)

4 Transfer to a serving dish and garnish with chilies and/or the coconut. Serve hot with rice and Cucumber Raita (see page 52).

Braised Lamb with Almonds

This dish is an excellent example of classic Moghul cooking, considered by many to be the most refined Indian cuisine. It is found in restaurants in both India and abroad.

SERVES 6

2lb/900g boned lean lamb
  shoulder or leg, cut into
  1in/2.5cm cubes
Juice of 1 lime
2 tsp salt
1 tsp freshly ground black pepper
1 tsp ground turmeric
2 cups/450g plain yogurt
4 tbsp vegetable oil
1 yellow onion, finely chopped
4 garlic cloves, crushed
2 tbsp fresh root ginger, peeled
  and finely chopped
10 green cardamom pods
2 tsp coriander seeds
2 cinnamon sticks
1 tsp chili flakes
2 tbsp slivered blanched almonds
1 tsp chopped fresh parsley or cilantro,
  to garnish

1 Place the lamb in a non-metallic bowl and squeeze the lime juice over it. Add the salt and pepper, and mix well, then stir in the turmeric and half the yogurt. Cover and refrigerate for at least 8 hours or overnight. Stir from time to time to redistribute the marinade.

2 Heat the oil in a heavy frying pan or flameproof casserole and sauté the onion over high heat for 2 minutes, or until soft. Add the garlic, ginger, cardamom pods, and coriander seeds and cook, stirring, for 1 minute.

3 Add the lamb and marinade to the pan and simmer gently for 10 minutes, stirring frequently. Add the remaining yogurt, cinnamon sticks, and chili. Simmer gently for 30–40 minutes, stirring frequently. Add a little water, if necessary.

4 When the meat is cooked, turn off the heat, remove the cinnamon sticks and discard. Add the almonds and mix well. Cover and leave to stand for 5 minutes. Transfer to a serving dish and sprinkle with parsley or cilantro. Serve with rice.

Pork Vindaloo

In their search for the New World,
Portuguese seamen discovered India and
left their cultural and religious marks
on Goa. The use of pork in Indian cuisine
goes back to their influence, and this
Goan curry is a delicious example.

SERVES 4–6

4 yellow onions, cut into quarters
8 garlic cloves
2in/5cm fresh root ginger, peeled
2 tbsp chopped fresh cilantro
4 fresh green chilies, seeded and sliced
1 tsp ground cumin
1 tsp ground cinnamon
5 green cardamom pods
1 tsp ground turmeric
2 tbsp vegetable oil
2lb/900g lean pork, cut into 1in/2.5cm
  cubes
1 (400ml) can unsweetened coconut milk
1 tsp sugar
2 tbsp cider vinegar
1 tsp tamarind pulp (optional)
Salt
2 tbsp chopped fresh cilantro and 2 tbsp
grated unsweetened shredded coconut,
  to garnish

1 To prepare the green masala, put the
onions, half the garlic, half the ginger,
and the cilantro in a food processor.
Process, adding a little water to form
a smooth paste. Set aside.

2 To prepare the yellow masala, put
the chilies, cumin, cinnamon, cardamom
pods, turmeric, and remaining garlic
and ginger in a food processor. Process,
adding a little water to form a smooth
paste. Set aside.

3 Heat the oil in a heavy frying pan or
flameproof casserole and fry the green
masala over high heat until brown. Add
the pork and cook, stirring, for 1 minute.
Add the yellow masala and cook for about
5 minutes, or until the pork is firm.

4 Add the coconut milk and bring to a
boil. Add 1 tsp salt, the sugar, vinegar, and
tamarind pulp, and mix well. Reduce the
heat and simmer, covered, for 1 hour, or
until the sauce is thick. Stir from time to
time, adding water if necessary. Adjust
the seasoning. Transfer to a serving dish
and sprinkle with cilantro and coconut.
Serve hot with rice and Cucumber Raita.

Chicken Tikka

Chicken tikka is sold by street vendors throughout India. These tikka kebabs can be made beforehand and will be that much better for the extra time they spend in their succulent marinade.

SERVES 6

6 chicken breast fillets, each cut into 8 pieces
1 yellow onion, coarsely chopped
3 garlic cloves, coarsely chopped
1in/2.5cm fresh root ginger, peeled
1 cup/240ml plain yogurt
2 tbsp toasted sesame oil
Juice of ½ lemon
3 tsp ground coriander
1 tsp ground turmeric
1 tsp chili flakes
1 tsp salt
1 yellow onion, cut into quarters and separated into layers

1 Place the chicken in a large non-metallic bowl and set aside.

2 Put the chopped onion, garlic and ginger in a food processor and process to make a smooth paste. Add the yogurt, sesame oil, lemon juice, coriander, turmeric, chili and salt, and process until smooth.

3 Pour the marinade over the chicken, toss to coat, then marinate in the refrigerator overnight. Stir from time to time to redistribute the marinade. Soak 12 bamboo skewers in water overnight.

4 Assemble the tikka kebabs. Thread four pieces of chicken on to each skewer, alternating each piece with an onion layer. Baste the kebabs with more marinade, cover, and return to the refrigerator until ready to cook.

5 To cook, prepare a barbecue, or preheat the broiler. Cook for several minutes on each side, turning once. Serve immediately with rice and a fresh salad.

Fish Caldine

Different versions of this tasty fish dish can be found in both northern and southern India. This recipe is from the Kerala coast.

SERVES 4-6

1in/2.5cm fresh root ginger, peeled
1 tsp ground cumin
1 tsp ground turmeric
1 garlic clove
1 (400ml) can unsweetened coconut milk
4 tbsp oil
2lb/900g firm-fleshed white fish, either
  whole or in fillets (scored three times on
  each side if using whole fish)
1 yellow onion, finely chopped
1 fresh green chili, finely chopped
1 tbsp whole cilantro leaves
Salt
1 chili, sliced lengthways, to garnish
1 lime, cut into wedges, to serve

1 Put the ginger, cumin, turmeric, garlic, and 1 tsp salt in a food processor and process to a smooth purée. With the motor running, add the coconut milk and process until smooth. Set aside.

2 Heat half the oil in a heavy frying pan and sear the fish for 2 minutes on each side. Carefully remove the fish and set aside. In the same pan, add the remaining oil and fry the onion and finely chopped chili together over high heat until the onion is soft and transparent. Return the fish to the pan. Add the coconut milk mixture and lower the heat.

3 Simmer gently for 10–15 minutes, basting the fish with the coconut mixture frequently, until most of the liquid has been absorbed. Adjust the seasoning.

4 Transfer the fish to a serving dish and sprinkle with cilantro leaves. Garnish with sliced green chili and serve with lime wedges for squeezing over. Coconut Rice (see page 53) makes an excellent accompaniment.

Buttered Greens with potatoes

This simple peasant dish will make a wonderful addition to any Indian meal. Serve as a side dish, or as part of a selection of dishes for an Indian buffet.

6–8 SERVINGS

1lb/450g fresh spinach (or 10oz/300g frozen spinach)
1lb/450g fresh chard, kale, mustard, or other greens
5 tbsp butter or peanut oil
1 tsp cumin seeds
2 garlic cloves, finely chopped
1 fresh green chili, seeded and finely chopped
4 firm potatoes, peeled and cut into quarters
1 tsp ground ginger
1 tsp garam masala or curry powder
Salt

Cook's Tip

You can use any combination of fresh greens for this dish. Just be sure that half of them are spinach.

1 Wash the fresh spinach and greens thoroughly. Drain well and pat dry. (If you are using frozen spinach, defrost and squeeze out all the extra water.) Chop the spinach and greens coarsely.

2 Heat the butter or oil in a large frying pan or flameproof casserole. When it is very hot, add the cumin seeds, garlic, and chili and stir-fry for 1 minute. Add the potatoes, reduce the heat, and brown all over for about 6 minutes.

3 Add the chopped spinach and greens in four batches, cooking each batch for 1 minute until wilted, before adding the next batch.

4 Sprinkle over the ginger and 1 tsp salt, and mix well. Add 1 cup/240ml boiling water. Reduce the heat and simmer, covered, for 20–25 minutes until the potatoes are tender.

5 Uncover and stir in the garam masala or curry powder. Cook for 5–10 minutes until all the moisture has evaporated, then adjust the seasoning and serve.

Carrot Halva

Indian desserts are very sweet and rich, so a little goes a long way. Here, carrots are transformed into a meltingly sweet luscious treat with raisins and nuts.

SERVES 6–10

2lb/900g carrots (preferably young),
  grated
4 cups/1 liter milk
1 tsp ground cinnamon
1 tsp ground cardamom
1 tsp ground turmeric
½ cup/120g butter
1 cup/225g light brown sugar
2oz/50g raisins
2oz/50g slivered blanched almonds
1 tsp rose water
4 tbsp chopped pistachio nuts or
  caramelized almonds, to serve

> **Cook's Tip**
>
> To make caramelized almonds, use the recipe in Prunes steeped in Tea and Vanilla on page 84.

1 Grate the carrots very finely and put them in a deep, heavy pan with the milk, cinnamon, and cardamom.

2 Bring the mixture to a boil, then lower the heat and cook gently over a medium-low heat for about 1 hour, stirring frequently, until the mixture has reduced by about half and most of the milk has been absorbed.

3 In a small bowl, dissolve the turmeric in 1 tbsp hot water. Stir into the carrots with the butter and sugar, and cook for 10 minutes, or until the mixture pulls away from the sides of the pan as you stir. Add the raisins and almonds, and cook for 5 minutes more.

4 Spoon the halva into a rectangular dish, smooth over with a spatula and leave to cool to room temperature. Serve in individual bowls with a dash of rose water and chopped pistachio nuts or caramelized almonds.

Masala Chai

This fragrant spiced tea can be served at any time of the day or with a spicy meal to soothe the taste buds. It goes very well with Carrot Halva.

SERVES 4

4 cups/1 liter water
1 cup/240ml milk
1 cinnamon stick
6 green cardamom pods
4 whole cloves
1in/2.5cm fresh root ginger, peeled and
  finely chopped
8 black peppercorns (optional)
4 tsp sugar
4 heaping tsp or 6 teabags of a
  full-bodied black leaf tea, such as
  English Breakfast tea

1 Pour the water and milk into a heavy pan and bring to a boil. Add the spices and sugar. Stir to blend and turn off the heat. Cover the pan and leave the spices to steep for at least 15 minutes.

2 Add the tea and bring the mixture to the boil. Turn down the heat, cover, and simmer for 5 minutes. Remove the lid and adjust the sugar and milk to taste. Strain into a teapot and serve in small cups.

4

Arabian Nights

Exotic flavors of the Middle East

Cold Turkish Yogurt Soup

Yogurt is actually a Turkish word, and it is said that it was the Turks who first brought yogurt to Europe. It is used in many of their dishes, including this simple and tasty cold soup.

SERVES 6

¼ cup/50g rice
2 cups/450g plain yogurt
2 tbsp flour
Juice of ½ lemon
1 tsp ground cumin
1 garlic clove, crushed
4 tbsp/50g butter
2 tbsp chopped fresh mint
2 egg yolks
Salt and freshly ground black pepper
6 mint sprigs and olive oil, to garnish
For the stock
1 carrot
1 leek, white only
1 celery stalk
1 garlic clove, crushed
1 onion, studded with 6 cloves
1 bouquet garni (1 sprig each of parsley and thyme, and 3 bay leaves)
4 whole peppercorns
1 tsp coarse salt

1 To make the stock, put the vegetables and flavorings in a large pan with 8 cups/ 2 liters water and bring to a boil. Cook for 30 minutes. Strain and discard the vegetables and flavorings, and add water to make up to 8 cups/2 liters.

2 Bring the stock to a boil, add the rice, and cook for 15 minutes over high heat. In a small bowl, whisk together the yogurt, flour, lemon juice, cumin, and garlic. Pour into the soup and simmer for 5 minutes.

3 Melt the butter in a pan, add the mint and sauté for 1 minute. Add to the soup, and remove the pan from the heat. Whisk the egg yolks into the soup. Add salt and pepper to taste, then chill.

4 Ladle the soup into bowls and add a mint sprig and a dash of olive oil to each one. Serve with Turkish bread and salad.

> **Cook's Tip**
>
> You can make this soup a day ahead and keep it in the refrigerator.

Kisir

This delicious bulgur wheat salad is the Turkish version of the classic Lebanese tabbouleh. The rich red bell pepper paste, which is available in Asian and Mediterranean stores, gives this salad its characteristic taste and warm color.

SERVES 6

1 cup/225g bulgur wheat
1 bunch green onions, trimmed and finely chopped
2 ripe tomatoes, seeded and diced
1 red bell pepper, seeded and diced
1 small cucumber, peeled, seeded and diced
1 small bunch parsley, chopped
4 tbsp chopped fresh mint
1 generous tbsp red bell pepper paste
½ cup/120ml olive oil
Juice of 1 lemon
1 tsp chili flakes
1 tsp ground cumin
½ tsp ground cinnamon
Salt

1 Put the bulgur wheat in a bowl, add 1 tsp salt and pour over cold water to cover. Leave to stand for 30 minutes. Drain off any excess water, then tip the bulgur wheat into a large salad bowl.

2 Add the green onions, tomatoes, and bell pepper to the bulgur wheat and toss together to combine. Add the cucumber, parsley, and mint, and toss again to mix.

3 In a separate bowl, mix together the red bell pepper paste, olive oil, lemon juice, chili flakes, cumin, and cinnamon.

4 Pour this mixture over the bulgur wheat salad and mix thoroughly. Add salt to taste and chill for at least 1 hour before serving. Serve as an appetizer or as a light meal with cold Chachouka (see page 75)

Piyaz

This classic white bean salad is found
throughout Turkey and Cyprus. It is
a staple dish, often served with Kofta,
in taverns in Istanbul.

SERVES 6

12oz/350g dried white kidney beans,
   soaked overnight in cold water, drained
   and rinsed
1 cup/225g green beans, cut into thirds on
   the diagonal
4 tomatoes, peeled, seeded and chopped
3 red onions, thinly sliced
1 tsp paprika
1 garlic clove, crushed
1 fresh green chili, cut into thin slices
4 tbsp chopped fresh parsley
1 lettuce
2 hard-boiled eggs, cut into wedges
12 black olives, to garnish
½ lemon, cut into 6 wedges, to garnish
Salt and freshly ground black pepper
For the dressing
4 tbsp olive oil
1 tsp cider vinegar
Juice of 1 lemon

1 Put the white beans in a pan, pour over
water to cover and bring to a boil. Skim
the surface and add 2 tsp salt. Cook for
about 1 hour, or until the beans are soft,
skimming the surface occasionally. Add
more water if necessary.

2 Drain and rinse the beans under cold
water and cool to room temperature. Put
in a salad bowl.

3 Steam the green beans for about
10 minutes, or until tender. Refresh under
cold water, then leave to cool and add to
the salad with the tomatoes and onions.
Add the paprika, garlic, chili, and parsley,
and mix well.

4 To make the salad dressing, whisk the
ingredients together and pour over the
salad. Season to taste.

5 Put the bean salad in a flat serving
dish on a bed of lettuce and add the
eggs and olives. Garnish with the lemon
wedges and serve as an appetizer or as
a side dish to accompany Kofta (see
page 78).

Chachouka

This spicy Tunisian version of the French classic, ratatouille, is cooked with eggs. Served with couscous, it makes a perfectly balanced light lunch or evening meal.

SERVES 4

4 tbsp olive oil
2 large onions, finely chopped
2 red bell peppers, seeded and cut into 1in/2.5cm pieces
1 yellow bell pepper, seeded and cut into 1in/2.5cm pieces
1 green bell pepper, seeded and cut into 1in/2.5cm pieces
8 large tomatoes, peeled, seeded and chopped
3 garlic cloves, peeled
1 small fresh green chili, seeded
1 tsp paprika
1 tsp ground cumin
2 tsp salt
1 tsp freshly ground black pepper
4 eggs
1 tbsp finely chopped parsley or cilantro, to garnish

1 Preheat the oven to 350°F/180°C/Gas 4. Heat half the oil in a heavy frying pan and sauté the onions and bell peppers over high heat until the onions are soft but not brown. Add the tomatoes and simmer uncovered for 20–30 minutes, or until all the liquid has evaporated.

2 Using a mortar and pestle or a food processor, purée the garlic with the chili, paprika, cumin, and salt and pepper. Stir the purée into the cooked vegetables.

3 Transfer the mixture to an ovenproof dish. Smooth the surface, then make four depressions with the back of a spoon. Break an egg into each depression and sprinkle the remaining oil evenly over the top of the eggs and vegetables. Bake for 10 minutes, or until the eggs are just set.

4 Sprinkle with parsley or cilantro and serve with steaming couscous.

> **Cook's Tip**
>
> To serve the dish cold, don't cook the eggs in the chachouka. Leave the vegetable mixture to cool, and hard-boil the eggs.

Stuffed Eggplant

Stuffed eggplant is the pride of Middle Eastern and Mediterranean cooking. There are vegetarian and meat-filled variations. This one is vegetarian.

SERVES 4

4 firm eggplants
½ cup/125ml olive oil for basting, plus
  2 tbsp for cooking
1 tsp coarse salt
2 tbsp raisins
1 large yellow onion, finely chopped
2 large tomatoes, finely chopped
½ cup/110g toasted pine nuts
1 tsp ras el hanout (optional)
½ tsp ground cumin
2 garlic cloves, crushed
2 tbsp chopped fresh parsley
Salt and freshly ground black pepper

> **Cook's Tip**
>
> Ras el hanout is a popular blend of spices, usually including cinnamon, nutmeg, ginger, pepper, cloves and dried rose petals. It can be found in Middle Eastern and Mediterranean stores.

1 Preheat the oven to 425°F/220°C/ Gas 7. Cut the eggplants in half lengthways, and place cut-side up in a baking dish. Rub generously with olive oil. Sprinkle with coarse salt and bake for 20 minutes until cooked through.

2 Remove from the oven and leave to cool. Reduce the temperature to 400°F/ 200°C/Gas 6. Using a spoon, scoop out one-third of the flesh from each eggplant, leaving a hollow; be careful not to pierce the skins. Chop the flesh and set aside.

3 Soak the raisins in hot water for about 10 minutes, then drain. Heat 2 tbsp of the oil in a heavy frying pan and sauté the onion over high heat until transparent. Add the tomatoes and raisins. Simmer for 10–15 minutes, or until the liquid has been reduced by half. Add the eggplant flesh, pine nuts, ras el hanout, cumin, garlic, and parsley. Remove from the heat and season with salt and pepper to taste.

4 Heap the mixture into the eggplant shells. Cover with foil and bake for 30 minutes, or until cooked. Serve hot with rice, or cold with a green salad.

Braised Spinach
with Raisins & Pine Nuts

This classic dish is popular throughout the Mediterranean—from Spain to Lebanon. Fruit is often used in savory Middle Eastern cooking, and here it is partnered with delicate pine nuts and rich, garlicky spinach.

SERVES 6

2lb/900g fresh spinach, stems removed
2oz/50g raisins
2oz/50g pine nuts
3 tbsp olive oil
1 garlic clove, crushed
1 onion, sliced
Freshly grated nutmeg
Salt and freshly ground black pepper

Cook's Tip

Frozen spinach is a convenient alternative to fresh in this recipe. Simply leave the spinach to defrost and squeeze out the excess water. There is no need to steam it.

1 Steam the spinach until it just starts to wilt. (Be careful not to overcook it.) Leave to cool slightly. When cool enough to handle, chop coarsely and set aside.

2 Put the raisins in a small bowl, pour over hot water to cover and leave to soak for 5–10 minutes, or until soft. Drain and set aside.

3 Toast the pine nuts in a heavy frying pan over medium heat, stirring constantly. (Watch them carefully, as they brown quickly.) Remove from the pan as soon as they are lightly browned. Set aside.

4 In the same pan, heat the oil and sauté the garlic and onion over high heat until the onion is transparent. Add the spinach and sauté for 3 minutes.

5 Add the raisins and pine nuts and toss to mix well. Add a pinch of nutmeg, and season with salt and black pepper to taste. Transfer to a serving dish and serve with boiled meat or fish.

Kofta

These classic Moroccan meatballs are also known as kefta and kufte. You can use a single type of ground meat but a mixture of beef and lamb is excellent.

SERVES 6

1lb/450g ground beef
1lb/450g ground lamb
2 yellow onions, finely chopped
1 tbsp paprika
1 tbsp coriander seeds
1 tsp salt
½ tsp freshly ground black pepper
1 egg
½ cup/50g fresh breadcrumbs
For the tomato sauce
3 tbsp olive oil
1 yellow onion, finely chopped
6 ripe tomatoes, peeled, seeded and
  chopped
1 tbsp ras el hanout (see page 76)
1 tsp ground cumin
1 tsp coriander seeds
1 cinnamon stick or ½ tsp ground
  cinnamon
1 tsp sugar
Salt and freshly ground black pepper
2 tbsp toasted sesame seeds, to garnish

1 Mix together the ground beef and lamb in a large bowl. Add the onions, paprika, coriander seeds, salt, and pepper. Stir in the egg, breadcrumbs, and 3 tbsp water until well mixed.Chill for about 3 hours.

2 Preheat the oven to 425°F/220°C/ Gas 7. Grease a baking dish.

3 Shape spoonfuls of the meat mixture into walnut-sized balls, and arrange in the baking dish. Bake for 15 minutes, or until lightly browned.

4 To make the tomato sauce, heat the oil in a large pan and cook the onions over high heat until transparent. Add the tomatoes, ras el hanout, spices and sugar, and stir in ½ cup/120ml water. Simmer for 20 minutes. Add 2 tsp salt and ½ tsp pepper.

5 Add the meatballs and any juices to the sauce and simmer gently for about 30 minutes. Remove the cinnamon stick, if using, and adjust the seasoning. Transfer to a serving dish. Sprinkle with toasted sesame seeds and serve with rice or couscous and your favorite hot sauce.

Chachi Kebassi

This dish, a variation of lamb shish kebab, is found throughout the Middle East. You can replace the walnuts with almonds to give it a typical Syrian touch.

SERVES 6

3 onions, finely chopped
1 tbsp paprika
1 tsp ground cumin
4 tbsp olive oil
Juice of 1 lemon
1 tsp salt
½ tsp freshly ground black pepper
2lb/900g lean boneless lamb (leg or
    shoulder), cut into 1in/2.5cm cubes
1 tbsp fresh chopped parsley or cilantro,
    to garnish
For the yogurt sauce
1 cup/225g yogurt
3 tbsp coarsely ground walnuts
Salt and freshly ground black pepper

1 Put the onions, paprika, cumin, olive oil, lemon juice, salt, and pepper in a food processor and process until smooth.

2 Place the lamb in a large, non-metallic bowl and pour over the onion mixture. Toss to coat each piece of meat well, then leave to marinate for at least 3 hours or overnight in the refrigerator.

3 To make the sauce, put the yogurt in a pan and add the walnuts. Heat gently until the sauce is just warm to the touch. Season to taste, and keep warm.

4 Thread the meat on to six metal skewers. Grill over charcoal or broil under a preheated broiler for 10–15 minutes, turning several times and basting with the remaining marinade.

5 Transfer to a serving platter and top the cooked kebabs with yogurt sauce. Garnish with parsley or cilantro, and serve immediately with rice and a fresh salad.

Tagine with Prunes & Almonds

A tagine is the conical clay pot that is traditionally used to make this North African stew. However, the term has come to describe any type of meat stew made with dried fruit and nuts. It is always seasoned with ras el hanout, a North African spice mixture, but you can replace it with your favorite curry spice mixture.

SERVES 6

3lb/1.3kg boneless lean beef or lamb, cut into 1½in/4cm cubes
4 tbsp ras el hanout (see page 76)
½ cup /120ml olive oil
4 onions, halved and sliced
3 cinnamon sticks
1 large white turnip, cut into ½in/1cm slices
1½ cups/350g prunes
3 garlic cloves, crushed
1 cup/200g toasted whole blanched almonds
Salt and freshly ground black pepper
2 tbsp fresh chopped cilantro or parsley, to garnish

1 Put the lamb in a large non-metallic bowl. Blend the ras el hanout with ½ cup/120ml water and pour over the lamb. Mix well to coat each piece of meat. Marinate for at least 3 hours in the refrigerator.

2 Heat the olive oil in a heavy frying pan or flameproof casserole and sauté the onions over high heat until they start to brown. Add the meat and cook until the pieces are brown on all sides.

3 Pour over water to cover, then add the cinnamon sticks and turnip. Simmer, uncovered, for 30 minutes, stirring occasionally so that the meat doesn't stick to the base of the pan. Add more water if necessary.

4 Stir in the prunes and garlic, cover the pan and simmer for 30 minutes until the meat is tender, stirring from time to time.

5 Season with salt and pepper. Sprinkle toasted almonds over the top, garnish with cilantro or parsley, and serve with steamed couscous.

Tunisian-style Tuna

The Mahgreb (Morocco, Algeria and Tunisia), with its long Mediterranean coast and its abundant varieties of fish and diverse cultures has given us many unique and delicious ways of preparing seafood. The use of fresh mint gives this dish an unusual twist.

SERVES 4

4 thick slices of fresh tuna,
  about 6–7oz/175–200g each
1 cup/120g flour
4 tbsp olive oil
20 fresh whole mint leaves
8 garlic cloves, slivered
2 bay leaves
½ tsp thyme
2 tsp paprika
2 fresh green chilies, cut in half
  lengthways
Juice 1 lemon
Salt and freshly ground black pepper
Mint sprigs, to garnish

1 Coat the tuna with flour. Heat half the oil in a heavy frying pan and sear the tuna for 2 minutes on each side. Remove from the pan and set aside.

2 Add the remaining oil to the pan and add the mint, garlic, bay leaves, thyme, paprika, chilies, and lemon juice. Cook over medium-high heat for 2 minutes.

3 Return the tuna to the pan. Add 2 tbsp water, then cover and cook over low heat for 5 minutes, or until the fish is heated through. (Don't overcook). Season with salt and pepper to taste.

4 Transfer the fish to a serving dish, garnish with mint sprigs, and serve with rice or couscous and braised spinach.

Prunes Steeped in Tea & Vanilla

This light and easy-to-make dessert is perfect for all seasons. The prunes are especially good served with vanilla or cinnamon ice cream, and topped with the crunchy almonds.

SERVES 6

36 large prunes
2 heaping tsp dark tea leaves (such as Ceylon or Assam)
½ cup/120g sugar
1 vanilla bean, split down the middle, or 1 tsp vanilla extract
Vanilla or cinnamon ice cream, to serve (optional)
For the caramelized almonds
1 cup/100g slivered almonds
¼ cup/50g white sugar

Cook's Tip

The steeped prunes can be stored in the refrigerator for several days.

1 To make the caramelized almonds, combine the almonds and sugar in a non-stick pan. Place over a high heat, stirring constantly, for 2–3 minutes. When the almonds start to brown, pour them into a heatproof dish. When they are completely cool, break them up. Set aside.

2 Soak the prunes in hot water for at least 2 hours, then drain. Transfer to a large heatproof bowl.

3 Boil 2 cups/475ml water in a pan and add the tea. Turn off the heat and leave to steep for 10 minutes. Strain and pour the tea over the prunes, then stir in the sugar and vanilla. Leave the prunes to macerate for 2–3 hours, then chill until ready to serve.

4 Serve the prunes cold, with a little of the tea mixture. Add a scoop of vanilla or cinnamon ice cream, if you like, and top with the caramelized almonds.

Baklava

This sweet and sticky dessert is found throughout North Africa and in every country around the Mediterranean basin. Sweet pastries such as these are not usually eaten as a dessert after a meal, but enjoyed as a treat with a small cup of hot, strong coffee or glass of sweet mint tea.

MAKES ABOUT 40 PIECES

1lb/450g pistachio nuts, walnuts, or
  toasted or blanched almonds
½ cup/110g toasted sesame seeds
  (optional)
1 tsp ground cinnamon
½ tsp ground cardamom
3 tbsp honey
1lb/450g filo pastry, thawed if frozen
1 cup/225g melted butter
2 tbsp chopped pistachio nuts, to
  decorate
For the syrup
1 cup/225g honey
1 tbsp lemon juice
1 tbsp orange blossom or rose water

1 Chop the nuts. Add the sesame seeds, if using, cinnamon, cardamom, and honey. Blend well and set aside.

2 To make the syrup, place the honey and ¼ cup/60ml water in a small pan and bring to a boil over medium heat. Cook for 10 minutes, or until the syrup thickens slightly. Add the lemon juice and orange blossom or rose water, and mix well. Remove from the heat and leave to cool.

3 Preheat the oven to 350°F/180°C/ Gas 4. Place 1 sheet of filo pastry in the bottom of a shallow 9 x 13in/23 x 33cm baking pan. Brush well with melted butter. Layer half the filo sheets on top, brushing each sheet generously with butter. Spread the nut mixture evenly over the last sheet, then layer the remaining filo pastry sheets on top, brushing each one with butter. Brush the top sheet with butter.

4 Using a sharp knife, cut small 2–3in/ 5–7.5cm diamonds, making sure to cut through all of the layers of the pastry. Bake for 40 minutes, or until puffed and light golden brown.

5 Remove the pastry from the oven and pour the cool syrup over the top. Leave the pastry to cool to room temperature.

6 Cut through the lines once again, sprinkle the pistachio nuts over the top and serve the diamond-shaped pastries with glasses of Moroccan mint tea or small cups of Turkish coffee.

> ### Cook's Tip
>
> • To make a more layered pastry, divide the filo sheets into three. Layer as before, but spread half the nut mixture between each third so that there are two layers of filling.
> • To make Moroccan mint tea to serve four, put 2 tsp or 2 teabags green tea in a warmed teapot and add 10 sprigs of mint, 1 sprig of absinthe (optional), and 3 tbsp sugar (or to taste). Fill the pot with boiling water and leave to steep for 3–4 minutes. Strain the tea into small glasses and decorate with a sprig of mint and pine nuts, if you like.

5

Fire & Spice

South-east Asia on a plate

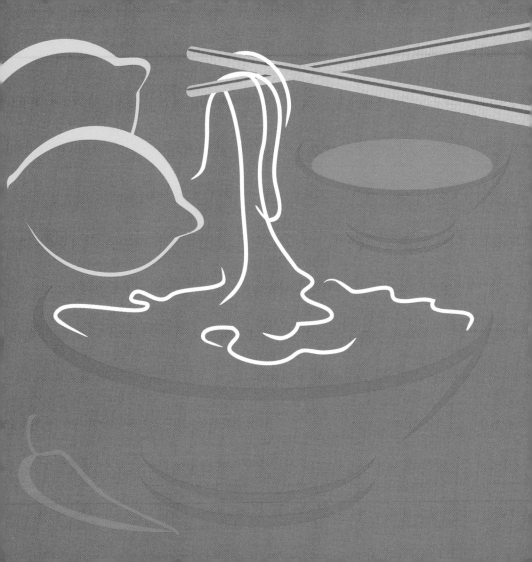

Green Papaya Salad

Ripe papaya has sweet, succulent orange flesh and is usually eaten as a dessert, but the green fruit is crisp and crunchy and can be used as a vegetable. It is particularly good in this classic Thai salad. Serve as one of a selection of dishes, or enjoy as a light meal with fragrant coconut rice. The more unusual ingredients such as dried shrimp and the Vietnamese fish sauce, nuoc mam, can be found in most Chinese and Asian markets and stores.

SERVES 4

1 green papaya (about 6oz/175g)
½ cup/115g green beans, cut into 1in/2.5cm
  pieces on the diagonal
2 garlic cloves, crushed
2 red or green chilies, seeded and sliced
1 tbsp dried shrimp
Juice of 1 lime
1 tbsp nuoc mam
1 tbsp sugar
2 tbsp coarsely chopped roasted peanuts
2 limes, cut into wedges, to garnish
2 fresh red chilies, thinly sliced, to serve

1 Cut the papaya in half lengthways. Peel and scoop out and discard the seeds. Use a hand grater or mandolin to make long shreds of papaya. Alternatively, use the coarse grater disk of a food processor.

2 Steam the green beans for 10 minutes; they should retain a definite crisp bite. Refresh under cold water and set aside.

3 Put the garlic, chilies, and dried shrimp into a food processor or blender, and process to make a paste, adding a little water if necessary. Set aside.

4 Put the shredded papaya in a salad bowl and toss with the garlic and chili paste, using a wooden spoon. Press the papaya into the sides of the bowl with the spoon until it is slightly softened. Add the lime juice, nuoc mam, and sugar, and mix well. The papaya should be slightly limp.

5 Add the cooked green beans, and toss to combine. Sprinkle with the peanuts and garnish with lime wedges and sliced chilies on the side.

Thai Eggplant with Tofu

Tofu—or tow hoo as it is known in Thailand—is a nutritious source of protein made from soya beans. Also known as beancurd, it is widely used in the Asian kitchen.

SERVES 4

8oz/225g firm tofu
1lb/450g eggplant
4 tbsp vegetable oil
1 tsp toasted sesame oil
2 garlic cloves, crushed
1–2 fresh red chilies, seeded and chopped
10–15 sweet basil leaves, coarsely chopped
2 tbsp yellow or black bean sauce
1 tbsp toasted sesame seeds, to garnish

1 Wrap the tofu in a clean dishtowel and place beneath a 2¼lb/1kg weight (a heavy frying pan filled with water will do). Leave to stand for 1 hour, then cut the tofu into 1in/2.5cm cubes. Cut the eggplant into ½in/1cm slices.

2 Heat half the vegetable oil in a wok or large pan. Add the tofu and stir-fry gently until brown on all sides. Work in batches so that the tofu does not break up. Remove from the wok and set aside.

3 Heat the remaining vegetable oil and sesame oil in the wok or pan. Add the garlic, and stir-fry for about 30 seconds, or until just light brown. Add the eggplant slices and cook for 5–7 minutes, or until cooked through, then add the chilies, basil, and bean sauce. Mix gently and cook for 1 minute.

4 Return the tofu to the wok. Cover, turn off the heat, and leave to stand for a few minutes, or until the tofu is warmed through. Transfer to a serving platter and sprinkle with toasted sesame seeds. Serve immediately.

Broccoli in Coconut Milk

In Southeast Asia, green vegetables are often cooked in coconut milk with spices. This dish can be served as a side dish, or with additional tofu or shellfish as a main course. Trassi or shrimp paste can be found in Asian stores.

SERVES 4

1lb/450g broccoli (preferably Chinese)
2 tbsp vegetable oil
1 yellow onion, finely chopped
2 garlic cloves, crushed
1in/2.5cm fresh root ginger, peeled and
  finely chopped
1 tsp ground turmeric
1 green chili, finely chopped
1 (400ml) can unsweetened coconut milk
2 tsp trassi or shrimp paste
1 lemon grass stalk, chopped
Juice of 1 lime
2 tbsp chopped cilantro or basil,
  to garnish

Additional ingredients

8oz/225g firm tofu, cut into bitesize
  pieces
8oz/225g fresh or frozen scallops or
  shelled shrimp

1 Cut the broccoli into small florets, and cut the stems into slices. Steam for about 5 minutes, or until just crisp. Refresh under cold water, and set aside.

2 Heat the oil in a wok or large pan, and add the onion, garlic, ginger, turmeric, and chili. Stir-fry for 5 minutes, or until the onion is transparent and the mixture starts to form a paste.

3 Add the coconut milk, trassi or shrimp paste, lemon grass, and lime juice. Cook over high heat for 5–10 minutes, or until the liquid has reduced by about one-third.

4 Add the broccoli and any additional ingredients, if using, and cook for 3 minutes, or until it is warmed through. Check the shellfish is cooked through, but be careful not to overcook the broccoli; it should still retain its bite. Transfer to a serving dish, and garnish with cilantro or basil. Serve with rice.

Thai Seafood Curry

Green seafood curries are a cross between a soup and a stew, and are the pride of Thai cuisine.

SERVES 6

2 tbsp vegetable oil
1 yellow onion, finely chopped
1in/2.5cm galangal or fresh root ginger, peeled and finely chopped
2 garlic cloves, crushed
2 tbsp green Thai curry paste
1 (400ml) can unsweetened coconut milk
1 fresh green chili, sliced
1 tsp turmeric
2 cups/475ml vegetable or fish stock
4 tbsp nuoc mam (Vietnamese fish sauce)
1 (425g) can bamboo shoots, cut into strips
1 tbsp sugar
Salt to taste
8oz/225g spinach, coarsely chopped
Juice of 1 lime
10oz/275g white fish fillets
10oz/275g raw jumbo shrimp, shelled and deveined
10oz/275g scallops
3 tbsp fresh cilantro leaves, to garnish
lime wedges, to serve

1 Heat the oil in a wok. Add the onion, galangal or ginger, and garlic and stir-fry for several minutes, or until the onion is transparent. Add the curry paste, coconut milk, chili, turmeric, stock, nuoc mam, bamboo shoots, and sugar. Cook over high heat for 10–15 minutes, or until the liquid has reduced by one-third. Reduce the heat and add salt to taste.

2 Working in batches, cook the spinach in the sauce for 1 minute. Remove with a slotted spoon and divide between six soup bowls. Add the fish fillets, shrimp, and scallops to the wok and cook for 2 minutes, or until the seafood is just cooked. Add the lime juice. Garnish with cilantro and spoon over the spinach. Serve with lime wedges and rice.

Cook's Tip

To shell and devein shrimp, plunge into boiling water for 10 seconds, then cool in cold water. Peel off the shell, leaving the tail intact. Make a shallow incision along the back of the shrimp and remove the black vein. Rinse and set aside.

Thai Grilled Lobster

This is a "far out" dish from a "far out" land for a special occasion. It is easy to prepare and will dazzle your guests.

SERVES 4

4 tbsp vegetable oil
4 garlic cloves, crushed
2 shallots, finely chopped
2 tbsp fresh root ginger, peeled
  and grated
3 tbsp nuoc mam (Vietnamese fish sauce)
Juice of 2 limes
1 tbsp honey or sugar
1 fresh red chili, finely chopped
2 lobsters, cooked and halved,
  claws removed
1 lettuce
1 bunch parsley
¼ cucumber, sliced
2 baby green onions, sliced
1 lime, cut into wedges, to garnish

1 Preheat the broiler. Heat the oil in a heavy frying pan. Add the garlic, shallots, and ginger, and sauté over high heat until golden. Add the nuoc mam, lime juice, honey or sugar, and chili to the pan, and heat through for about 10 seconds.

2 Place the lobsters on the broiling rack, cut side up, with a pan beneath to catch any juices. Spread the ginger mixture evenly over the lobster and broil for 3–4 minutes, or until heated through.

3 Line a platter with lettuce, parsley sprigs, and cucumber slices, and place the lobster on top. Sprinkle with sliced green onions and garnish with lime wedges. Serve at once with a side dish such as Green Papaya Salad (see page 91).

Pho

This beef noodle soup is a meal in itself, and is probably the most widely eaten dish in Vietnam—sold by street vendors from Saigon to Hanoi. There are many variations, but the traditional version always contains beef and rice noodles, which are known as pho.

SERVES 6

8oz/225g lean boneless beef (sirloin)
12oz/350g flat rice noodles
6 cups/2¾ pints beef stock
2 tbsp finely chopped fresh root ginger
1 tbsp lime juice
2 whole star anise
½ tsp black peppercorns
1 cinnamon stick
¼ cup/60ml nuoc mam (Vietnamese fish sauce)
1 cup/150g fresh bean sprouts
2 whole green onions, chopped
2 tbsp fresh cilantro or basil leaves, and 1 thinly sliced fresh red or green chili to garnish (optional)
2 limes, cut in wedges, and Hoisin sauce to serve

1 Put the beef in the freezer for about 30 minutes until very firm but not frozen. Cut the meat into very thin slices across the grain. Set aside.

2 Cook the noodles in boiling water for 5 minutes, or until soft. Rinse under cold water and set aside.

3 Put the beef stock, ginger, lime juice, star anise, peppercorns, cinnamon stick, and nuoc mam in a large pan and bring to a boil. Reduce the heat and simmer for 20 minutes. Strain and bring to a boil. Add the bean sprouts to the stock and cook for 1 minute, then remove using a slotted spoon and set aside.

4 Working in three batches, poach the beef in the stock for 1 minute. As soon as the meat has changed color, divide the beef among six serving bowls. Divide the noodles, bean sprouts, and green onions among the bowls. Pour the hot stock over the top and sprinkle cilantro or basil and chili over each bowl. Serve with lime wedges and Hoisin sauce.

Indonesian Chicken Soup

**This fragrant coconut soup contains
galangal, a member of the ginger family.
It has a slightly lemony flavor when
young, becoming more peppery with age.
It is widely used in Indonesian cooking.**

SERVES 6

3 cups/750ml chicken stock
1 (400ml) can unsweetened coconut milk
1 tsp freshly ground black pepper
1 tsp ground turmeric
4 lemon grass stalks, chopped
3in/7.5cm fresh galangal or ginger root,
  peeled and cut lengthways into paper-
  thin strips
1 kaffir lime leaf, rolled and thinly sliced,
1 fresh red chili, thinly sliced, or ½ tsp chili
  flakes
2 chicken breast portions (5oz/150g),
  finely sliced
4oz/115g fresh firm white or shiitake
  mushrooms, sliced
1 (425g) can bamboo shoots, cut into
  fine strips
1 tbsp sugar
Juice of 1 lime
4 tbsp nuoc mam (Vietnamese fish sauce)
12oz/350g noodles, cooked (optional)

For the garnish
1 whole green onion, thinly sliced
2 tbsp fresh cilantro leaves
1 kaffir lime leaf, shredded
1 fresh red chili, thinly sliced, or ½ tsp
  chili flakes

1 Heat the stock and coconut milk in a
large pan with the black pepper, turmeric,
and lemon grass. Add half the galangal
or ginger, the lime leaf, and chili. Boil for
15 minutes, then strain and reheat.

2 Add the chicken, mushrooms, bamboo
shoots, and sugar to the stock, and
simmer for 5–10 minutes, or until the
chicken is cooked through.

3 Add lime juice and nuoc mam to the
soup, and simmer for 2 minutes. Add the
noodles, if using, then spoon the soup
into individual bowls. Garnish with green
onions, cilantro, kaffir lime leaf, and chili,
and the remaining galangal or ginger.
Leave to stand for several minutes before
serving, either as an appetizer or as a
main meal with an accompaniment such
as Green Papaya Salad (see page 91).

Lamb & Shrimp Satay

Satay is a traditional Indonesian kebab that is generally prepared with pork or chicken, and served with a spicy peanut sauce. Our lamb and shrimp satay brings this dish to another level of elegance.

SERVES 6

1.5lbs/700g lean boned lamb (shoulder or
   leg), cut into 1in/2.5cm cubes
24 raw jumbo shrimp
vegetable oil, for basting
½ cup/110g chopped peanuts, to garnish
Rice and Indonesian peanut sauce,
   to serve
For the marinade
2 tbsp dark soy sauce
2 shallots, chopped
1 garlic clove, chopped
1 tbsp lemon juice
½ cup/120ml unsweetened coconut milk
1in/2.5cm galangal or fresh root ginger,
   peeled and finely chopped
1 tbsp curry powder
½ tsp freshly ground black pepper
1 tsp honey
1 tsp ground cumin
1 tsp ground coriander

1 Put the lamb in a non-metallic bowl. Blend the marinade ingredients in a food processor, then add the paste to the lamb. Mix well, and marinate overnight in the refrigerator. Soak 12 bamboo skewers in cold water overnight.

2 Prepare a barbecue or preheat the broiler. Alternate 2 pieces of lamb with one shrimp on the skewers and baste with oil. Cook for 3 minutes on each side. Garnish with peanuts and serve with rice and peanut sauce (see below).

Cook's Tip

To make the sauce, heat 4 tbsp peanut oil in a frying pan. Add 2 finely chopped shallots, 2 crushed garlic cloves, and 1in/2.5cm grated galangal or root ginger. Fry until the shallots are translucent. Add 1 tbsp curry powder and stir for 1 minute. Add ½ cup/120ml water, 1 (400ml) can coconut milk, 1 tsp shrimp paste, juice of 1 lemon, 2 tbsp honey, 2 tbsp light soy sauce, and ½ cup/110g smooth peanut butter. Simmer for 10 minutes, adding more hot water if necessary.

Rice Vermicelli
with Pork & Vegetables

Rice was the traditional staple of Indonesia and no meal was complete without it. Noodles were introduced by the Chinese, adapted by the Indonesians, and have become the second staple of their cuisine.

SERVES 4

12oz/350g rice vermicelli
12oz/350g mixed vegetables (such as
  broccoli, snow peas, and asparagus)
1 tbsp arrowroot or cornstarch
1 tsp honey
½ cup/120ml chicken or vegetable stock
4 tbsp vegetable oil
4 tbsp light soy sauce
2 garlic cloves, finely chopped
1in/2.5cm fresh galangal or ginger root,
  peeled and finely chopped
8oz/225g lean pork, sliced into thin
  1in/2.5cm squares
1 tbsp nuoc mam (Vietnamese fish sauce)
1 tbsp black bean sauce
1 tbsp chopped basil leaves or cilantro,
  to garnish

1 Cook the noodles according to the instructions on the packet. Rinse under cold water and set aside.

2 Prepare the vegetables: cut broccoli into florets; cut snow peas in half; cut asparagus into 2in/5cm pieces. Steam the broccoli and asparagus for 5 minutes until tender but still crisp. Refresh under cold water and set aside.

3 Blend the arrowroot or cornstarch and honey with the stock. Set aside. Heat half the oil in a wok and add the noodles and 1 tbsp soy sauce. Stir-fry for 30 seconds, then transfer to a serving platter.

4 Add the remaining oil to the wok. Stir-fry the garlic and galangal until they start to change color. Add the pork and snow peas, and stir-fry until the pork starts to brown. Add the remaining soy sauce, the nuoc mam, black bean sauce, vegetables and stock mixture. Stir until the sauce thickens, then pour over the noodles and garnish with basil or cilantro.

Sticky Black Rice Pudding

with Coconut Sauce

No Thai meal is complete without a
dessert. This one is a real show-stopper
with its distinct nutty flavour and
exotic appearance.

SERVES 8

1½ cups/250g black glutinous rice
½ cup/120g light brown or palm sugar
1 (400ml) can unsweetened coconut milk
1 small cinnamon stick
1 tsp salt
4 eggs
2 tbsp unsweetened shredded coconut
For the sauce
3 egg yolks
⅓ cup/75g sugar
2 tbsp flour
½ tsp salt
1 (400ml) can unsweetened coconut milk

1 Rinse the rice well in cold water, then
put in a bowl, pour over cold water to
cover, and leave to soak for at least
8 hours, and preferably overnight.

2 Put the rice and 2 cups/475ml water
into a pan and add half the sugar, half the
coconut milk, the cinnamon stick, and the
salt. Bring to a boil. Turn down the heat
and simmer for 30 minutes, stirring
frequently, until the rice is tender and
most of the liquid has been absorbed.
(The mixture should not be dry.)

3 Remove the pan from the heat, cover,
and leave to cool for at least 30 minutes.
(The rice can be prepared up to a day in
advance.) When the rice is cool enough,
remove the cinnamon stick and discard.

4 Preheat the oven to 350°F/180°C/
Gas 4. In a large pitcher, whisk together
the remaining coconut milk, sugar, and
eggs and pour over the rice, mixing well.
Spoon into a heatproof soufflé dish or
eight individual ramekins.

5 Place the soufflé dish or ramekins in a roasting pan and pour 2in/5cm water around the dish or dishes. If using a soufflé dish, bake for 30 minutes, or until the custard has set; if using ramekins, bake for 20–25 minutes. Remove from the oven and leave to cool.

6 When the custard is cool, run a sharp knife around the edge of the dish and shake the custard loose. Unmold a large custard on to a serving plate or individual desserts into bowls. Sprinkle shredded coconut over the top.

7 To make the sauce, whisk together the egg yolks, sugar, flour, and salt in a bowl until the mixture starts to become slightly thicker and paler. Heat the coconut milk in a pan until just boiling, then remove from the heat.

8 Gradually pour the hot coconut milk into the egg mixture, stirring constantly to prevent lumps forming. Pour the mixture back into the pan and heat slowly for 5–7 minutes, stirring constantly, making sure that the mixture doesn't stick to the bottom of the pan.

9 As soon as the mixture reaches boiling point, remove from the heat and pour into a clean bowl. Leave to cool, stirring from time to time so that a skin does not form on top. Serve the sauce with the custard.

> **Cook's Tip**
>
> This is a great dessert for entertaining because you can make the custards and sauce in advance and simply turn the desserts out of their dish or dishes when you're ready to serve them. When using individual ramekins, they look very pretty served in their dishes if you don't want to turn them out.

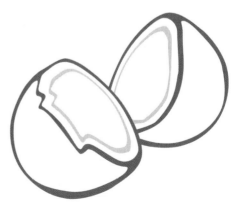

Mango Sorbet

This mango sorbet is easy to make and offers a light and refreshing finale to any meal. Although this recipe uses fresh mango, you can use canned or frozen instead.

SERVES 8

2 cups/450g sugar
1 vanilla bean, split lengthways
2 cups/450g mango, fresh, canned, or frozen, peeled and chopped
Juice of 1 lime
2 tbsp crystallized ginger, chopped, to garnish
Mint sprigs to decorate

1 Pour 2 cups/475ml water into a pan and add the sugar and vanilla. Bring to a boil and simmer for 2 minutes.

2 Remove the pan from the heat and leave to cool completely. When ready to use, remove the vanilla bean, split it, and scrape down the inside. Put the seeds into the syrup and discard the bean.

3 Put the mango in a blender and purée, or mash well by hand. Add the lime juice and vanilla syrup, and mix well.

4 If using an ice cream maker, follow the manufacturer's instructions to make a sorbet. If making by hand, pour the mixture into a freezerproof container and freeze for 4 hours. Beat in a food processor until smooth and then return to the container and freeze again.

5 When firm, scoop the sorbet into bowls and top with crystallized ginger. Decorate with a mint sprig, and serve with Coconut Sauce (see page 104) and Almond Cookies (see page 47).

Weights and measures

The following conversions and equivalents will provide useful guidelines for international readers to follow. There's just one golden rule to remember when you're preparing your ingredients: always stay with one system of measurement—that way you'll achieve the best results from these recipes.

Liquid ingredients			Dry ingredients		
½ tsp	=	2.5ml	¼oz	=	10g
1 tsp	=	5ml	½oz	=	15g
1 tbsp.	=	15ml	³⁄₄oz	=	20g
2 tbsp	=	30ml	1oz	=	25g
3 tbsp	=	45ml	1½oz	=	40g
¼ cup	=	60ml	2oz	=	50g
⅓ cup	=	80ml	2½oz	=	65g
½ cup	=	125ml	3oz	=	75g
⅔ cup	=	160ml	3½oz	=	90g
¾ cup	=	180ml	4oz	=	115g
1 cup	=	250ml	4½oz	=	130g
1½ cups	=	375ml	5oz	=	150g
2 cups	=	500ml	5½oz	=	165g
3 cups	=	750ml	6oz	=	175g
4 cups	=	1 liter	6½oz	=	185g
5 cups	=	1.2 liters	7oz	=	200g
6 cups	=	1.5 liters	7½oz	=	215g
8 cups	=	2 liters	8oz	=	225g

9oz	=	250g
10oz	=	275g
11oz	=	300g
12oz	=	350g
14oz	=	400g
15oz	=	425g
1lb	=	450g
1¼lb	=	500g
1½lb	=	675g
2lb	=	900g
2¼lb	=	1kg
3–3½lb	=	1.5kg
4–4½lb	=	1.75kg
5–5¼lb	=	2.25kg
6lb	=	2.75kg

Measurements

¼in	=	5mm
½in	=	1cm
¾in	=	2cm
1in	=	2.5cm
1½in	=	4cm
2in	=	5cm
2½in	=	6.5cm
3in	=	7.5cm
4in	=	10cm

Glossary

The following glossary of culinary terms will provide useful guidelines for international readers to follow.

all-purpose flour: plain flour
baking soda: bicarbonate of soda
bok choy: pak choi
broiler: grill
broil: to grill
Chinese cabbage: Chinese leaves
cilantro: coriander
collard greens: spring greens
cornstarch: cornflour
eggplant: aubergine
green bell pepper: green pepper
green onion: spring onion
ground pork: minced pork
jumbo shrimp: tiger prawn
litchis: lychees
red bell pepper: red pepper
shredded coconut: desiccated coconut
shrimp: prawn
slivered almonds: flaked almonds
yellow bell pepper: yellow pepper
vanilla bean: vanilla pod
vanilla extract: vanilla essence
zucchini: courgette

Index